THE ATTORNEY AUTHORITY REBOOT

(How, in 6 months, Attorney Geller added $74k in new clients, and boosted his AVVO rating to 10.0, using one simple strategy)

by **Richard Jacobs**

Speakeasy Publishing
73-03 Bell Blvd, #10
Oakland Gardens, NY 11364
www.speakeasypublishinginc.com

Ordering Information:

Quantity sales. Special discounts are available on quantity purchases by corporations, associations, and others. For details, contact the publisher at the address above.

Orders by U.S. trade bookstores and wholesalers. Please contact Speakeasy Publishing: Tel: (888) 991-2766 or visit www.speakeasypublishinginc.com.

Printed in the United States of America.

Published in 2017.

ISBN: 978-1-946481-04-7

FOREWORD

As the old saying (modified) goes: "If I had a dollar for every time someone told me they wanted to write a book for years, but never got around to doing it", well...you know the rest.

When I look back on the past 7 years of running and growing Speakeasy Publishing and Speakeasy Marketing Inc, I can safely say that 80% of these companies' revenue comes from potential clients reading my 1st and 2nd edition of "Secrets of Attorney Marketing Law School Dares Not Teach".

If I hadn't taken the time to write this book (and the 2nd edition, updated for 2017), these businesses would be a shadow of the tremendous success they are today.

Take heed, and get your book done - the sooner the better. I don't just say this in the hopes that you'll become our client and help us make a profit, I say it because I am living proof that writing, publishing, and promoting a book for your customer base is the single best thing you can do to grow your business and differentiate yourself from your competitors.

To your success,

Richard Jacobs
Speakeasy Marketing, Inc.
Speakeasy Publishing
July 1st, 2017

DEDICATION

To Dan Kennedy, a mentor, who inspired me to write my first book and has helped me understand the power of direct marketing.

To Lewis Bassett, a wise-beyond-his-years friend, mentor, and colleague, who provides much-needed polish to my presentations.

WARNING & DISCLAIMER

The intent of this book is to be informational in nature only.

Marketing techniques described herein may be found to be unethical by your local or State Bar Association, or they may be prohibited under local, state, or federal laws – it's your job to check this.

Laws change and times change. You must do your due diligence to ensure that following any of the marketing techniques in this book will not cause you legal or tax problems, or put you in conflict with your local or State Bar Association. No legal or tax advice is being given by the author, publisher, or anyone associated with this work.

Publisher, author, and all parties associated with this work are unaware of any material conflicts or issues that the implementation of these marketing techniques described herein may have or cause. This book is purely informational in nature, not to be taken as an instruction manual.

The effectiveness of the techniques described in this book cannot be guaranteed, especially if implemented improperly or half-heartedly. The techniques may boost your sales, have no effect, or even hurt your sales. The author and all parties involved in this publication take no responsibility for any outcome if you choose to use this material.

For legal advice, consult a qualified attorney. For tax advice, consult a qualified tax professional.

TESTIMONIALS

"Great Ideas On Marketing! You Hit The Nail On The Head."

"I have just finished reading your book and I have to say I am impressed with your marketing ideas. I have been in private practice, criminal and domestic, for about 3 years and have gone through many different marketing plans, schemes, and downright thefts that have occurred by some organizations that promise the moon and deliver nothing.

I have tried lead generators, SEO, billboards, pay per click and direct mail marketing. Most have failed miserably. I agree with your assessment that slower but effective plans work better. Big trees need big roots. I have already changed my firm's approach and have begun to see the payoff.

You hit the nail on the head with your tracking advice. In looking back on three years of trial and error I realized I could have dumped bad ideas faster once I realized they were not working. Lesson learned, and now we are tracking the source of our leads.

I found your advice on answering the phone and scripting particularly helpful. The ability to hear my staff's interactions with clients is crucial to seeing which staff member is better at handling new prospects. I have made my staff read that section to improve customer service. It is not just the lawyer who needs to change but the whole staff needs to be on the same page.

I keep your book by my desk and constantly refer to it as a source for new ideas. Turning a talk into a book is next on the agenda and hope to have a new one linked to the website soon. Thanks for the ideas!"

- David E. Boyle, Esq.

****

"Great, Logical Marketing Tips That You Wouldn't Think Of"

"This was an excellent book on marketing. And a very quick read - took me a day. Not quite "secrets", but many tips in here that seem like common sense after you read it. Richard has done an amazing job spelling things out in the book. After reading it, I actually made an appointment to speak with Richard about how he could help my site. I loved his no-nonsense attitude in the book and during our meeting. He is a straight-shooter and doesn't really fluff.

One of the other reviews mentioned that the book was a lot of fluff and the book could be boiled down to 10-15 pages, but I disagree. I think the "fluff" is extra information that I believe is helpful to allowing the reader to perform these tasks on their own. Highly recommended. I've even given a few colleagues my copy to read."

- Matthew Murillo, Esq.

****

"Get The Book, Read It, Call Richard, and Have A Conversation"

"This book provided me with some new or better ways of marketing my law practice than what I've been doing for the past 20 years. I read, tabbed and made notes prior to visiting with Richard Jacobs by phone this afternoon, so as not to waste any of his time. You should know that not once did the subject of money come up in our conversation. Still, we'll have to get around to that eventually because I'm sure he's not a non-profit company.

The book is an easy read and really shares relevant information on different ways to reach the consumer. It discusses SEO, mailers, etc. and perhaps even more importantly, how you track whether it's making you money. I'm looking forward to our next conversation!"

- ***Denis H. White, Jr., Esq.***

****

"Excellent And Practical Marketing Concepts I Recommend This Book"

"As an attorney in practice for over 25 years, I have studied and incorporated a number of marketing tools and approached for my practice. I have also worked with a few marketing companies. As such, I was interested to check out and read through the book. The concepts and points made in the book are excellent.

The author, Richard Jacobs, takes a practical approach to the marketing of a law firm. Many of the concepts presented can be incorporated immediately and some will take some time to implement but are certainly achievable. I recommend this book."

- David Wolf, Child Injury Lawyer

****

"Great Strategies For Legal Marketing"

"Richard's knowledge of attorney marketing goes far beyond any of the other legal marketers we have ever worked with. His book reveals marketing secrets that have provided tremendous benefit to our firm. He has his finger on the pulse of the legal markets and this book was a tremendous help for our marketing needs."

- Marc Grossman, Esq.

****

"Unless You Have More Law Business Than You Can Handle, You Need This Book!"

"I consider Mr. Jacobs' book to be one of the more practical and useful books on Marketing for Attorneys that is out there. It is chock full of easy to understand and implement practical ideas and roadmaps for increasing an attorney's business, especially for sole practitioners and small law offices business.

Unless you do not care about increasing your income from practicing law, this book is for you! The best part of reading Mr. Jacob's book is that it is written in a way that is enjoyable and fun to read and put to immediate use. It is the opposite of "dull!" Get this book!"

- Robert H. Tourtelot, Esq.

****

"Outstanding. Enjoyed It."

"I don't think I ever gave a review for a book. The book is short and well written. This guy is outstanding. I really enjoyed reading because I enjoy the business aspect of marketing law firms. When I first started practicing law, the yellow pages ran things. Now that Google balanced the playing field, this guy explains how to compete with Google. I get at least one SEO guy a week trying to sell me something; this is the first guy I can say that actually knows what he is talking about. I still have not hired him to handle my stuff but when I am ready (still learning) this is the guy I will go to."

- Mark Rollins, Esq.

****

"Interesting and Practical Guide To Growing Your Law Business"

"Whether you're just starting your law practice or have been practicing for years, this book is a terrific resource for practical marketing ideas. Mr. Jacobs lays out how customer service and smart SEO can grow your law practice. He also outlines how easy it can be to add a large volume of quality, relevant content to your website, thereby boosting your organic SEO. This book will force you to examine and reconsider your marketing if you are serious about increasing your business and growing your practice."

- Amy Chapman, Esq.

****

"Real Advice For Real Attorneys That Gets Real Results"

"Real advice for real attorneys that gets real results. Richard's book is starkly different than most of the marketing advice out there for attorneys. It is targeted at smaller firms and solos and really attacks the problems faced by these entities.

Definitely worth a read and the ideas will stay with you and become a significant part of your marketing mix. An extra bonus is the author's accessibility and willingness to answer any follow up questions you have. It's nice to see a professional so focused on the success of his clients."

- Josh Reinitz, Esq.

****

"A Good And Quick Read With Several Actionable Ideas To Grow Business"

"I thought this was a great book. It really gave me several things to think about in terms of growing my practice. He sets forth concrete and actionable ideas. They are straightforward, legal and if you think about it truly make sense.

It's a wonder so many of us have missed them through the years (or just refuse to make the effort). You're given the choice whether to implement them yourself or use the author's firm. I'm still deciding how to proceed but regardless there are great ideas in here that when put into practice can't help but increase business."

- Gabriel Katzner, Esq.

****

TABLE OF CONTENTS

About The Author

Richard Jacobs specializes in helping attorneys break free from 70 hour work weeks and marginal law practices. Through his work at Speakeasy Marketing, Inc, he helps hundreds of attorneys nationwide transform their lives, bank accounts, and law practices into successful, revenue producing businesses.

Richard began in 2009 building myDUIattorney.org from scratch and growing into a nationwide advertiser for DUI attorneys. He now helps hundreds of solo practitioners, and small law firms of 2 to 20 attorneys in 17 different practice areas (including Family Law, Personal Injury, Criminal Defense, Immigration and more) learn, implement, and profit from sound marketing that law school dares not teach.

Richard is the author of three books:

- "But I Only Had 2 Beers!"
  (Truth Talk from Over 25 DUI Lawyers)
- Secrets of Attorney Marketing Law School Dares Not Teach (1st and 2nd Editions)
- The Ultimate Guide to Local Business Marketing (Published by Entrepreneur Press; Richard Jacobs (co-author)

Richard has spoken about Law Firm marketing at:

- NACDL Las Vegas DUI Conference (Private session held during the conference)
- PILMMA (Personal Injury Lawyers Marketing & Management Association)
- DUIDLA Arizona Conference
- Perry Marshall & Associates Small Business Marketing

If you're ready to improve your law practice and break free of mediocrity & struggle, contact Richard Jacobs today at Speakeasy Marketing, Inc. at www.SpeakeasyMarketingInc.com or (888) 225-8594.

Chapter 1
The Attorney Authority Reboot

In this book we are going to talk about how in six months Attorney Paul Geller landed $74,000 in new cases and achieved a 10.0 AVVO rating using one simple strategy. You will discover the biggest issues facing attorneys in 2017 and why it's going to put hundreds of small firms out of business. You are also going to learn the simple strategy that helps you retain more clients, charge a higher fee and build a moat around your practice just like the one Warren Buffett talks about building. The how and why of the strategy is going to boost your AVVO rating and earn you more Google and Yelp reviews. You will also discover the seven specific credibility claims attorneys think increases their perceived status but actually commoditizes them and in some cases hurts their reputation.

You will also discover a short phrase you need to add to your business cards, your website and to your emails so you can close more potential clients and elevate your perceived status. If you can relate to any of these statements below, this book may be the most important thing you have read in a long time:

1. You are worried about AVVO and other directories that train potential clients to compare you to other attorneys like apples in a supermarket. They encourage potential clients to price shop law firms, which no one likes.

2. You may be frustrated by juvenile attorneys that are cutting their prices to the bone and their desperation for business makes them willing to cut their own throat, and yours, right along with them. The problem here is getting worse. There are too many freshly minted attorneys created every day for each new case or job that comes along.

Are You Sick Of Wasting Time And Free Advice On Potentials?

Are you sick of wasting time and free advice on potential clients that ignore your phone calls and go on to hire someone else? Or worse yet, the ones that come back to you with a low-ball price the other attorney offered and ask you to match it? It's an insult. Do you want to increase the number of new cases that you get each month? Do you want to charge higher fees and work with clients who are a better fit for your long-term goals? If so, then pay attention. In this book I am going to show you how to do just that with a genuinely simple strategy.

Additionally I am going to show you seven different ways to further leverage the strategy with you to attract better clients in 2017. There is another bonus. There are going to be some real life examples of how other attorneys have implemented what I'm going to tell you about so you can see how it's done.

Chapter 2
THE BIGGEST PROBLEM THAT SMALL LAW FIRMS AND SOLO ATTORNEYS FACE IN 2017

So what is this book NOT about? It's important to talk about this. It's not another SEO trick or growth hack. It's not some monthly marketing subscription plan that will start working in just three more months. It's not about spamming people or bothering potential clients or sending direct mail. It's not about promoting your firm in an unprofessional or unethical way that will upset your state or local bar association.

To begin, I have a question for you. What do you consider to be the biggest problem that small law firms and solo attorneys are facing in 2017? The biggest problem that I see lawyers facing in 2017 is actually commoditization.

Competition, as you know is increasing again. Graduating law school students are multiplying like flies. Many attorneys, as you know, are sadly cutting their prices to the bone, hurting themselves and hurting you in the process. Legal Zoom, Rocket Lawyer and AVVO are encouraging clients compare you to competitors. Sadly they are fostering price shopping and commoditization. The average client nowadays, who used to get a second opinion, now can evaluate seven different attorneys at one time. As the old saying goes, you can't ride a horse with two asses. The same thing applies here; a client can only hire one attorney.

What does that say about competition? Some attorneys love AVVO, Rocket and all of those websites and they do get business from them. Some get business from their profiles while others pay to advertise. A lot of attorneys hate these services though because of what they are doing to the market. However you feel about AVVO, Rocket Lawyer and Legal Zoom, they are hugely successful. They are big companies that are making a lot of money. Love them or hate them, they are doing something right. Legal clients especially love them because they get all their information in one place. Additionally AVVO, Rocket, Legal and other similar sites know something most attorneys don't. If more attorneys did know this, these services would really have no attraction and wouldn't get anywhere.

Chapter 3

What Do AVVO, Rocket And Zoom Understand About Clients That Most Attorneys Don't?

What do you think AVVO, Rocket Lawyer and Legal Zoom understand about clients that most attorneys don't? In my experience here is what these companies understand: Clients don't know how to choose the right lawyer. They are scared and overwhelmed because they are in a bad legal situation. They are drowning in information, in reviews, in different attorneys, articles to read, etc. They are lazy yet they are impatient. They want answers and they want help right now but they are barely able to do a search on Google and spend five seconds reading an article sometimes.

You also have this bad combination along with interruptions in the real world like Facebook, phone calls, text messages, Instagram, etc. People have a short, goldfish-like attention span. There are tons of competing firms just a mouse click away on Google or a touch away on smart phones. You can look up attorneys in literally a second. AVVO, Rocket and Legal Zoom, serve up 10 attorneys on a page, further commoditizing them and they make them look all the same with a standard profile. Here is what a typical AVVO search might look like and based on that, which attorney would you choose if you had a problem.

Below are three more profiles showing the same thing.

What do you notice about this? They all use the same credibility claims and none of these claims enhance their perceived status. The reason is because every attorney uses the same claims which actually commoditize you and everyone else that uses them.

Chapter 4
Credibility Claims That Don't Mean Anything Anymore

Here are seven specific credibility claims that unfortunately don't mean a thing anymore. This is taken from the "Unique Lawyer Dollar Menu", or in other words AVVO:

1. "I have 20 years' experience." Count how many lawyers on AVVO have 20 years' experience. There are a lot of them.
2. "I'm aggressive. I'll fight for you." That doesn't really mean anything. No attorney is going to claim to be a wimp.

3. "I'm a former prosecutor," or "I'm a former public defender." So what? There are a lot of people with this experience.

4. "I'm board certified," or "I'm a Million Dollar Advocate." You may understand what that means and the work that went into it but potential clients don't. They don't know what a Million Dollar Advocate is or what board certified means and it doesn't really impress them.

5. "I'm available 24/7." Room service is available 24/7. People of high stature are not. On demand people that you pay $5 an hour, they are available 24/7 so that claim actually hurts you.

6. "I graduated from Harvard Law School or Cornell Law School." Clients don't really know much about law schools. Everyone has to graduate from law school otherwise you wouldn't be a lawyer; so nothing special there.

None of these reasons mentioned above, these assertions, these credibility claims, give the potential client a motivation to choose you versus another attorney.

Chapter 5
Here Is What Happens When You Commoditize Yourself

You look and sound just like everyone else so now getting clients becomes a numbers game. That's a game you don't want to play. Potentials pick from the "McLawyer Dollar Menu". Sometimes they will choose you. However, you won't be able to command high fees and you probably will have to offer a discount or a payment plan otherwise they will go on to the next attorney on the list. No good. You've seen some of this with your clients and your potential clients, I'm sure.

Nod your head if you know what I'm talking about. I'm not making this stuff up. So what's the solution to commoditization? Authority. Become the most authoritative attorney in your metro and in your practice area.

Here is what an authoritative attorney looks like from the point of view of the client: David will be our hypothetical person. He was arrested for DUI in California, the same state as (real attorney) Attorney Paul Geller that I mentioned earlier. He is a mid-level manager for a Fortune 100 company. If he is convicted of DUI, he is going to lose his job. His wife may divorce him and he might not live with his kids anymore. His community will probably disown him. His friends won't respect him anymore. Everything is on the line for this guy.

Now if you were in David's shoes, which attorney would you choose to save your life and your career? This attorney or this one? What about this one? How about this one? Would you choose this attorney?

Chapter 6
Write A Guidebook For Potential Clients

The most powerful way to build your authority as an attorney is to write a guidebook for potential clients. Unlike other attorneys, Attorney Paul Geller is not a commodity. For someone in California who is looking for a DUI lawyer, he becomes the obvious choice. In fact, some clients are even willing to pay a premium to work with his firm because he literally wrote the book on fighting DUI charges in California.

So who would you rather hire? An attorney who is available 24/7 or the published author of "Arrested for DUI in California: Useful Information to Help You Fight Your DUI Case"?

Now you may be thinking, "I've been planning to write a book for years now. It's been on my list but I just don't have the time." Can you relate? If so you are going to find that what I'm about to show you is very interesting and useful. Attorney Geller used this strategy to land $74,000 in new cases in six months but here is the thing: It didn't take him six months of work. Although his book is 100% his own words and ideas, he didn't actually write a single word of it. He used the method that I'm about to share and it took him just three hours in total to get the whole thing done. By the way, Attorney Geller doesn't just specialize in DUI. He actually wrote three books on various practice areas that he works in including DUI, sex crimes and other various criminal charges.

Attorney Geller is the preeminent authority in all of these practice areas and authority is everything. It's the key to attracting more clients and getting them to pay higher fees.

Chapter 7
Seven Ways To Get You More And Better Quality Cases

Here are seven ways that Attorney Paul Geller leverages his authority to consistently get more and better quality cases to boost his AVVO rating and to attract positive reviews. You too can use these tactics. They are free and I'm going to share them with you:

METHOD 1:

You want to use your book as a lead magnet and make it available for download on your website. On the left side of your page you should have an icon with the picture of the book, where you can click to download. On the right there should be a little form that pops up where visitors can enter their name, email and phone number. From there they can download the guide right away once they put in that information. What does this do? It turns the potential client into a lead that you can contact back by phone or email and someone you can engage with. It also gives them a non-threatening way to start getting your information without ever having to call you first.

There are many people that are timid about calling law firms and rightfully so. There are lawyers and law firms that are off putting when people call and this makes people nervous and uncomfortable. Making the book downloadable is a great way to give people another path that's not as scary to get the information they need and to start perceiving you as authority.

METHOD 2:

Next, you want to publish your book on Amazon and Kindle so that you are a bona fide published author. For example, Attorney Geller's book is on Amazon and has accumulated reviews. This is a great thing to be able to tell potential clients. Imagine saying, "I am a published author on Amazon and Kindle. You can buy my book there or I can send it to you for free."

METHOD 3:

You can both mail and email your book to potential clients. I would mention it to all prospects that call, even those who are a sure thing. You should tell everyone; from referrals to your best friend; it doesn't matter. You want to mention the book even to potentials who have an in office appointment. People commonly no-show so you should always be telling anyone you come into contact with about it. Also ensure your staff is also talking about it. Every single prospect should receive a copy of your book. If you can't afford or believe you can't afford to mail it to everyone then only mail it to people who show genuine interest. Everyone else should at least get an emailed copy.

If you can mail it, should send it using UPS Ground or Fed Ex 3 day - anything that says "open me". Sending potential clients your book really impresses people. They start to think, "Hey, this guy spent a lot of money to send this to me. It must be important. I'll open it."

Everyone needs a reminder to take action. Getting someone to consume this book, whether it's for two minutes or

30 seconds, is key to turning the potential into a paying client. Again, this is why getting a physical copy in their hands or emailing a copy several times (or even emailing chapters) is important. Getting the potential to receive the book in the mail or by email, getting him or her to open the package and flip through it, is a whole other animal than just telling someone about it on the phone. That's a lot more engaging.

Additionally, when you send out a book, include a personal letter. Chances are you do that anyway when a client signs on, so why not add an additional letter talking about the book, testimonials and other important information. It really makes a big difference.

METHOD 4:

Give the book to potential referral partners and use it to build a referral network. This means handing it to anybody who interacts with your customer before, during or after the time that you have met with him or her. This could include insurance companies; doctors; other lawyers in ancillary practice areas; financial planners; CPAs; mechanics; body shops; personal trainers; bail bondsmen and beyond. Give multiple copies of your book to your referral partners. Keep them stocked and replenished so that they don't ever run out.

By doing this, you are actually doing your referral partners a favor. It makes them look good to their clients because they can give them information that helps their situation.

For example, let's say there is a bail bondsman and he happens to have a copy of your book on DUI in his office. A client comes in to discuss bond matters. Now, the bondsman can't directly recommend your services. However, he might mention your office had provided this book as a free resource. Guess who that guy is going to call when he leaves his bondsman's office? Some random attorney out of the phone book? Or will he be calling you, the author of this book he was given as a gift. It makes a big difference. The same example could be applied to a body shop or a chiropractor. It doesn't matter who it is. This method works. It makes your referral partners look good. When they look good, you look good. Everyone is happy and everyone gets more business.

METHOD 5:

Turn your book into an email series, a video series or an audio series. Remember, getting potential clients to consume the material is key to your success. Different people consume content in different ways. Some prefer to watch and learn, whereas others like to listen. Others may prefer to read information. You must cater to all learning styles using this advanced tactic. If you do this, you will get a lot more people to actually read the book, mentally pay attention to it and in the end, you will get more clients that way.

Another tactic is to "chunk" the information together or turn it into byte sized pieces because the whole book may be too much to consume. It could be two sentences that make all the difference and then boom. That could be the little tidbit that leverages the authority or the power of your book in the mind of the reader. The whole goal here is to apply "Chinese water torture", so to speak, to your prospects. Warm them up slowly. Get them to remember you and to buy from you or in other words, get them to retain you. In the same way Chinese water torture works, it is a process of dripping the information onto the prospect. After awhile they can't take it anymore and they want to take action. Drip, drip, drip. The prospect is thinking, "I get your emails. I get your calls and your books. Alright I'm going to call you up and hire you."

METHOD 6:

You want to mention your author status as often as you can. Put it in your email signature and your email series. Put a picture of you holding a copy of your book on your website. Mention it on LinkedIn, AVVO, Yelp, Google+ and Thumb Tack. Feature it on your media pack or on your one sheet. Let's say you are soliciting local news or blogs to write articles on you. If you write a book, they are much more likely to pick you up. I have a client, Attorney Stephen Cobb, who practices in Florida. We just did a press release on a book we did with him and local news media picked it up. Now we are re-approaching that media and using that article for other media. We are also going to try and get him on the local news.

Additionally you should mention your book in your biography box, the "About Us" section or the attorney profile pages on your website. Your entire staff should be talking about it to potential clients. This includes your secretary, other attorneys, your answering service; anyone that touches potential clients. It's the best way.

METHOD 7:

When talking about local media we are referring to local newspapers, blogs, radio, etc. They are all looking for stories. If you send these outlets your book with one sheet of what it's about, what you can talk about on the radio or in a blog, they will pick it up. You can do press releases, bloggers may blog about it, again local TV, radio or newspaper may pick you up. Once that happens, now you've even got more credibility pieces and can promote "As seen on KPRT TV", "As seen on News 11", or maybe "As seen on Californialawblog.com" and those types of things. You should also mention if you end up speaking at industry conferences, which may or may not get you any business from the actual conference. However, if you appear as a speaker at various events it again gives you attention and credibility. There is NACDL, PILMA, NASCA, National Trial Lawyers Association and AVVO conference just to name a few. These are great places that are looking for authoritative speakers.

Authoritative speakers have books and therefore, you need to have one too. In the end, authority is everything and the best way to become an authority in your metro or in your practice area is to write the book just like Attorney Geller did. Again, being an author is the ultimate authority. The most powerful thing you will be able to put on your business card or on your AVVO profile, is "published author" of "book title here". It's a simple phrase that really changes the game because most attorneys won't ever publish a book, even if they want to. Why? Because writing a book is typically like eating an elephant. Even if you cut it into small chunks, it's going to take you a long, long time.

Chapter 8

Speak A Book -- Fastest And Easiest Way To Author A Book

So how did Attorney Paul Geller do it? How did he write three solid books that made him the authority in his metro and in his practice area, spending only three hours on each? Here is how: Speak A Book is the fastest and easiest way to author a book without writing a single word.

Attorney David Katz, of Katz & Philips in Orlando explains how this works. He has created a number of books using this method. Writing all of these books would have taken years or they probably wouldn't ever have been written had he not used the Speak A Book approach. After three re-prints of a DUI book alone, we can conservatively attribute a six to one return on money spent. My suspicion is that it's far higher than that.

A testimonial direct from Attorney Katz explains, "Becoming a published author has added to our brand and helped build our reputation among potential clients and other attorneys."

Speak A Book Process

Here is how the Speak A Book process works.

STEP 1:

We do a 30 minute strategy session by phone where we agree on the title and the premise. Here we flush out the high level content and what each chapter is going to be about.

STEP 2:

We do the deep dive phone interview. It's a relaxed and recorded 90 minute phone interview; not a deposition. This is specifically designed to extract your methodology and your ideas in a way that's structured and coherent. We then write the draft manuscript by transcribing that call. Our team removes all of the "umms" and the "ahhhs" and verbal artifacts. We then rearrange the content so that it has a good, structured flow.

The next step is where we will design your professional book. We dress it up with a professional design including a disclaimer; a table of contents; table of figures; an index; the front and back covers; publishing information; the ISBN; the barcode, etc. The book is then published on Amazon and Kindle and promoted and you are given physical printed copies as well. It will also be put on your website and for some attorneys, they may want to do audible.com for audio books.

The total process takes 30 days of our time, yet only three hours of your time and here is what you get at the end: You will get a PDF of your book that you can email to prospects and you can put it on your website for download, etc. You will have your own Amazon author biography page and your own kindle pages.

You will also get 200 printed copies shipped straight to your office that you can give out to your referral partners, prospects, etc.

How much would it cost you if you hire a ghostwriter to author your own book? I emailed a few of them to find out. In a comparison, I found out it would cost between $19,000 and $35,000 to do so. Here is the thing though: If you were to hire a ghostwriter, it wouldn't really be your book. It would be someone else's copycat ideas; someone who doesn't even have a law license or who doesn't have the years of experience that you do.

Considering that a mid-range ghostwriter charges about $25,000, we could easily charge the same thing for this but we don't. The Speak A Book service is a better value. We are not even asking half of that. Forget about it. Usually we charge $4997 for this service, but for readers of this book I'm offering a much better deal. First though, there is something important I have to share with you: Speak A Book is the fastest and easiest way to author a book without writing a single word.

Here is just a quick overview again of the process: Step one is the initial strategy session; Step two is the deep dive interview; Step three is the manuscript writing; Step four deals with the design and dressing and Step five is when we publish and promote the book. Again, you get the PDF copy and the download widget for your website, the Amazon and Kindle pages and a crate of 200 physical books to give out. The total process takes 30 days.

Here is my offer for you: I'm not going to ask you to pay the typical $4997. You are going to pay a discount and you don't even need to pay it all now. Contact us at (888) 225-8594 or email rj@speakeasymarketinginc.com and pay a $500 deposit and this will lock in your place.

Remember the strategy session is the first step in the process and if at the end of that call, you are not excited about the book or if you have any doubts, just let us know and we will refund your $500 and give your spot to another attorney. It's not a problem. No hassle, no hard feelings.

In full disclosure, we've done about 180 books and we have had two refund requests which were honored. No problem. We move on. End of the story. If you are satisfied and want to proceed, at the end of the strategy session we will ask for the remaining payment of $3437. In total you will pay $3997 instead of $4997. That's $1000 less than the normal price. If you want to spread the cost over two months, you can pay by phone and at the end of the strategy session, $1947. The second payment of $1947 will be charged after the book is delivered and is ready to get you clients.

Again, all you pay now is $500 as a refundable deposit. Remember with this process, it's your book. There are no strings attached. You own all the copyrights and you can order re-prints anytime you like from us or your own print house. There are no lock-ins, no additional expenses or subscriptions or anything like that.

I want you to imagine what your practice will look like when you are a pre-eminent authoritative attorney. Just like Attorney Geller, you could see a $74,000 lift in business over the next twelve months. The only downside is you will need new business cards and you might need to make a few tweaks to your website and will want to upgrade your AVVO, Yelp and Google+ profiles etc. But these are all good problems, right?

We can make you a bona fide published author in 30 days by helping you to create your own book; 100% of it being your words and your ideas. It's owned by you. This is a real book with an ISBN, a cover and you have physical copies that you can give out to potential referral partners, potential clients, etc. The best part is that other than taking a few hours, this strategy requires no work or time from you. You don't have to manage anything and you don't have to think about it. You just show up for the initial strategy call and then the interview call. Let us use our proven process and you reap the rewards.

Chapter 9
QUESTIONS & ANSWERS

Note: the following Q&A is taken from a live Q&A session, presented by Richard Jacobs, in 2017:

"You talked a lot about DUI during the session and you had a website that provided DUI leads. Do you only work with DUI lawyers?"

Richard Jacobs: No. Actually I mentioned earlier on that I've worked in and continue to work in 17 different practice areas. We've helped our attorney clients create books on family law, personal injury and auto accidents, immigration, workers' compensation and more. Again as I mentioned, we have created 180+ books. I don't know how many practice areas we've covered total in those books but at least 17 different topics. This means, it doesn't really matter what area of law you practice in. We've even done a few books for doctors, pain management, stem cells and that kind of thing. However, 95% of the books we've done are for attorneys in 17 different practice areas.

"In 90 minutes, how much content can you create?"

Richard Jacobs: We've found that 90 minutes is the "Goldilocks" length it takes to create a book of 60 to 80 pages. Some people say it's too thin or too flimsy. Some people say it's too thick and that no one will read it. We call it the "Goldilocks" length because literally it's just right. It's thick enough that it's actually a book but it's thin enough so that it's not intimidating. It's not like reading 'War and Peace' or the dictionary. It's a great size. Again it's just thick enough to be a real book but not too big where the shipping is too expensive and it's also not intimidating to the recipient. This book size is ideal because it can be consumed in an hour, sometimes two. That's why we keep it to the length that we do.

"My clients don't appear to be big readers. How will a book work for them? No one is going to read the whole thing."

Richard Jacobs: We get this all of the time and it refers back to what I said earlier. Here is a simple script your office can use with a potential client who calls in once your secretary or admin has gathered a few facts: "Alright I'm going to transfer you to Attorney Smith but before I do, just to let you know, she has recently written a book on divorce matters in Florida. It's a really great read and it's pretty short. It's on Amazon right now for $19 but she has asked us to offer a complimentary copy to anyone who calls the office and needs some information on a pending divorce. I'd like to offer that to you. What's your best mailing address and your best email address? We'll get it sent to you now via email and then we can get it out in the mail to you right away as well?"

The potential client generally responds with something like, "Oh, Attorney Smith has written a book? That's great! Here is my email address and mailing address!"

This is a simple script that you can use anytime someone calls your office. The person will perceive it as a gift. Some clients will tell the attorneys that they read the whole thing. Some clients will tell the attorneys that they were thinking about hiring someone else but they saw the book sitting on their kitchen table or they thought about the book. They didn't have time to read it but they really like the fact that it got sent to them and they decided to hire the attorney anyway. Some read it cover to cover while others flip through the pages for a second. These are all of the anecdotes I have heard. So, in seeing the act of being offered a book, getting the book by email and/or physically maybe even just holding it, looking at it for two seconds or flipping through a few pages - that alone has tremendous impact on a potential client.

It's not always enough to convince someone to hire you but for a large number of people it is. Don't think the person has to read the whole thing. Most of the time, they won't. They may go to one chapter that really concerns them because their case has a similar fact pattern to it. However, I have heard first hand that the books work even when someone is just looking at the cover.

"You say the book interview takes 90 minutes but yet the attorney has to spend 3 hours total. Why is that?

Richard Jacobs: The interview is 90 minutes but once we get you the first draft, you are going to want to look at it, make a few edits and that kind of thing. That will take typically maybe an hour of your time to dig into it a little bit and make sure it's looking good. The best attorneys will do that quickly and get it out the door. They don't want to get bogged down at that point so usually by spending an hour looking everything over, you are good to go. Therefore, the "3 hours" we are talking about is not a whole chunk of 3 hours; rather approximately 30 minutes and then 90 minutes with the interview and last some final editing and boom - you are done. We don't want to make it seem like it's a lot more than it is or a lot less than it is.

"Richard, great session. I learned a lot but I don't know if this is for me. I tend to convert almost every client that comes into my office. So how will this help me?"

Richard Jacobs: I love this question - it's a softball. I'm sure most attorneys will say that, once they get a client in the office, they almost always get the client to hire them, but getting a client into the office is never 100% guaranteed. There is a thing called the "no-show rate" on appointments and for some people it's as high as 50%. That aside, nowadays people are mobile. They don't necessarily walk in your door. They may want to close over the phone. Either way, if you don't cut down your no-show rate, even if you convert every single person that walks in your door, that's a bad thing. The book will definitely cut down on all of these problems.

You need to look at the client acquisition process as a funnel, as a path. The first time a potential client calls, the first point of contact is when someone in your office answers the phone. Second, depending on if you offered the book or not, even if the person says, "Okay thanks for the information. I'm going to call around and I'm going to call you back," chances are you will actually get more of those people because if you've mentioned or sent the potential a copy. You lose people at this critical stage and you may not even realize it.

Then there is the appointment stage: If you are good enough that you get a potential client in for an in office appointment or a later phone appointment, you don't necessarily close them right then. Again, there are no shows. When someone gets off the phone with you, all kinds of doubts start to creep in. They may talk to their mother who says "Why are you going to hire that guy? Hire Uncle Bob. He can work with you," for example. Or perhaps something like, "Can you even afford a lawyer?" or "Maybe you should just settle."

All of these things weigh on a person's mind. You have to realize that first phone call to your office is a scary phone call for anyone, even if it's just for a traffic ticket. No one wants to call a lawyer. The truth is, they are calling your office because they are getting a divorce or there was a death in the family or some other horrible event has taken place.

All of these decisions to talk to a lawyer are fraught with emotion and fear. That's why this book is so helpful. In this process, you may not even know you have all of these stages and you are losing people all along the way. The book helps patch the holes and that's why it can make you so much more money.

"Rich, at $4000 to do a book, it seems like it may or may not be worth it. How can you justify this price?"

Richard Jacobs: What is the value of a low end case for you? If you are a family law attorney, it could be $4000 or $5000; $3000 at the least. If you are a DUI attorney, it's $1500 or $2000. For attorneys who handle auto accident cases, you generally won't touch a case for under $10,000 on the one third split, at least. There is value in what you do. You know that and the great thing is once you have your book, you can raise your fees. We'll get into that shortly actually.

Getting back to the price, if your book lands you two new cases over the course of your entire career, this book will pay for itself.

You saw the testimonial from Attorney David Katz and as he mentioned he saw a six to one return. You must consistently use your book; actually use it, don't let it sit in the corner gathering dust and mention it to people.

You probably don't care but just letting you know, in my business, Speakeasy Marketing, Inc., I've sold $1000 worth of my books at Amazon. I've given away several thousand copies of my book over the years. It's made the company a lot of money. It's probably 80% of what really built the business for me. I'm living proof that it works.

This thing is real. If you use it you will be far better off. You will have less no shows. You will get more clients coming back to you. You will make money on it and if you really think you won't, then simply don't do the book.

The bottom line is that this is something you need to do and it will make you far in excess of what it costs. This will be like a splash in a pan based on what you can do with it in a year or two years.

"The laws in my area are changing. How can I address that in my book?"

Richard Jacobs: Interesting. We've had this happen. So how long does the book last you? Ninety percent of the book, maybe even 95% it will last you at least 3 or 4 years, maybe 5. Then, if there is a piece of legislation that changes, unless it's radical or a complete overhaul which rarely happens, you can always put an insert in your book so you can do a second edition years down the road.

Several of my clients have come back and done second editions and a lot of re-orders years later. I haven't really heard a single problem where the book was inaccurate and they couldn't use it anymore. I literally have yet to hear that. Therefore, I wouldn't worry about that kind of thing.

"My clients tend to be very online savvy, sophisticated. I don't think reading a book is their style. How can we do this online or use social media instead?"

Richard Jacobs: Everything is online. The good news, however, is that now physical is prized a lot more than it was. There is actually a book that came out, "The Revenge of Analog" where the author talks about this very thing. Direct mail, physical books or all these physical experiences actually are having a much greater effect because all those channels are less crowded. Everybody is online. Everybody thinks online is the end all be all and that is another reason why our books actually works better now than years past.

I'm not sure if you are aware but Amazon released statistics and they said that book consumption is way up. What people are tending to do is buy the book physically and read it on Kindle at the same time. There is this hybrid learning going on. They said physical book sales are actually up, not down. So don't believe the hype that everything is online and it's all social media. It's not. These physical books really work well and may cut down on over 10,000 emails that you could send. Believe me. It's a real big deal.

I hear from attorneys, "Rich I got your book in the mail. I read the whole thing cover to cover. Now what can you do for me?" If you go to Amazon, I have "Secrets of Attorney Marketing Law School Dares Not Teach", 1st and 2nd editions. The book has been instrumental in growing my business.

For yourself, like I just said, the book is huge. If you want to incorporate social media, you can do that. There is nothing wrong with it. Instead of just posting "Law Firm XYZ handles DUIs and Theft charges" on Facebook, Twitter or Instagram, you can instead mention your offer for your free book on social media. You could post something like, "Facing Divorce in Texas? Get this free book on how to survive with your sanity and your family intact." That will be much more likely to get you clients than a typical ad that has you standing in front of the law books with your arms folded, looking serious, listing your practice. Keep in mind the commoditizing claims we talked about earlier.

Imagine now instead an ad which shows you and the book and mentions the free book offer. You are going to look very different from everyone else and you have a much better chance of getting the business.

"We have three partners. Should we put the book in all of our names, the firm name or just one person's name?"

Richard Jacobs: Okay, great question. The good thing is that once the book is written, it can be put into all three; the firm's name, one of the partner's names, or all three. Everyone can have the book written by them using separate covers, titles, but the same content in pdf copies. There is nothing wrong with that. As long as each person has contributed at least somewhat, it's an honest practice. The most important thing that you want to come across is that the book is written by a person, not a firm. Potential clients are not hiring your law firm. They are hiring you, John Smith. They are hiring your personality and based on their interactions with you, how they feel about you, if they are confident in you, etc. It's a person to person interaction.

You've got to remember that in all of your marketing and especially with this. They want to hire the best at X and the best person that does X is you. Your book should come from you. It should have your picture on it because it builds more rapport. There are even more things that we can go into there but definitely coming from you is the most important part.

"How will having a book allow me to raise my fees? Clients already struggle to pay the fees."

Richard Jacobs: Great question. Like I said, talk about your book. Have everyone talk about it and prepare the potential clients when they get on the phone. When someone calls have your front office person get the facts of the case and mention the book.

"Alright I'm going to transfer you to Attorney Smith. Just so you know, he just finished a book called, 'How To Get The Most Money Out Of Your Auto Accident In South Carolina.' It's a great book. It's on Amazon usually for $15. The attorney wants you to have it for free. What's your best email address and physical address? I'll have it sent out to you right away."

Generally the potential client will appreciate it. Even if he or she says, "No thanks", there will be much less price resistance because they won't have heard this from any other attorney that they call. When shopping elsewhere the potential is going to hear the same gunk. Therefore, in their mind, you'll be just like all the other attorneys unless you talk about this book and make yourself stand out. You'll be really uniquely positioned and that is a whole different conversation. My clients tell me they literally hear the difference in a person's voice and they get badgered far less for payment plans because the person who walks in knows that this person is a badass, an authority. There is no talk of discounts and payment plans. This really helps and the great thing is it helps before they even utter those dreaded words to you. That's how it will help you to actually charge more and to get it without having to fight tooth and nail.

That concludes the Q & A portion. The bottom line is let's get this thing done. Get on board now because if you don't, months from now you will say the same thing you've said for 5 years. "I want to write a book. I'm just waiting until this trial is over." "I'm just waiting for the Messiah to return." "I'm waiting for this, I'm waiting for that."

It will never get done this way. Trust me. The years will go by. You will still be in the same place that you are in now and you'll be frustrated. The time to take action is now.

Get it done now. Get it out there. Get more clients. Make more money in 2017 and beyond. Get out of the inferior position of begging for clients, and living off of payment plans many clients never finish.

It's time to Speak your book!

WHAT SHOULD BE YOUR NEXT STEP?

Schedule a complimentary phone strategy session where we can hash out a compelling book title and get you started on the 30 day process of speaking and publishing your book.

Yes - in 30 days from now (literally), you can have your new book, done, and on its way back to you from the printers, listed for sale on Amazon and Kindle, and ready to start getting you new clients.

Call (888) 225-8594 or email rj@speakeasymarketinginc.com to schedule your complimentary phone strategy session today.

ACKNOWLEDGEMENTS

To Dan Kennedy, a mentor, who inspired me to write my first book and has helped me understand the power of direct marketing.

To Lewis Bassett, a wise-beyond-his-years friend, mentor, and colleague, who provides much-needed polish to my presentations.

OTHER BOOKS PUBLISHED BY SPEAKEASY PUBLISHING

1. How To Cope With The Aftermath Of An Auto Accident

Armando R. Payas, Esq. (Payas, Payas & Payas, LLP)

2. Commercial Vehicle Collisions In Texas

W. Bradley Parker, Esq. (Parker Law Firm)

3. Your Guide To Road Cycling Safety In Colorado

Bryan S. VanMeveren, Esq. (VanMeveren Law Group, P.C.)

4. Defending College Students Charged With A Sex Crime In Michigan

Daniel T. Geherin, Esq. (Simon & Geherin, PLLC)

5. Estate Planning In Wisconsin: Privacy, Protection And Taking Control

Daniel J. Krause, Esq. & Nelson W. Donovan, Esq. (Krause Donovan Estate Law Partners, LLC)

6. How To Live & Die With California Probate

John B. Palley, Esq. (Meissner Joseph & Palley, Inc.)

7. Reflections From Decades Of Practice In Personal Injury Law

Robert I. Feinberg, Esq. (Feinberg & Alban, P.C.)

INDEX

Notes